Sarah The Caterpillar

Reading Book 1-10

+ MacAdam Visual Media +

Integrated Learn To Read Program   English
Programme Intégré de l'Apprentissage de Lecture   Français

Sarah The Caterpillar Program Copyright 2015
Concept Louise Pierlot MacAdam
Written & Illustrated by Louise Pierlot MacAdam
Illustrations contributed by Charles MacAdam,
                    Alexander MacAdam
Illustration Concepts: Gregory MacAdam

All the images are in black and white.

Summary of the Program

Sarah The Caterpillar Reading Book
40 Stories of 6 pages each divided into 4 volumes
70 pages each volume

Sarah The Caterpillar Workbook
40 lessons divided into 4 volumes;
one lesson corresponds to one story
in the **Reading Book**.
80 pages each volume

Sarah The Caterpillar Key Word Book
20 pages in light weight carton
40 images in two sizes
of letters and letter group phonemes.

My Pictures and Stories
Supplementary workbook for the child's
own drawings and stories.

Vocabulary
240 words and derived words.
The Word List appears on the end page
of the **Reading Books**.

Programme Simone La Chenille Copyright 2015
Concept Louise Pierlot MacAdam
Écrit et Illustré par Louise Pierlot MacAdam
Illustrations contribué par Charles MacAdam
                    Alexander MacAdam
Concept d'illustrations: Gregory MacAdam

Toutes les images sont en noir et blanc.

Résumé du Programme

Simone La Chenille Livre de Lecture
40 Histoires de 6 pages divisé en quatre volumes.
70 pages chaque volume.

Simone La Chenille Livre Cahier
40 Leçons divisé en 4 volumes;
un leçon correspond à une histoire
dans le **Livre de Lecture**.
80 pages chaque volume

Simone La Chenille Livre Les Mots Clefs
20 pages en carton leger
40 images en deux grosseurs des lettres et
des groupes de lettres formant des phonèmes.

Mes Tableaux et Histoires
Cahier supplementaire pour ses propres
dessins et histoires de l'enfant.

Vocabulaire
230 mots et mots dérivé.
Voir la Liste des Mots à la dernière page
des **Livres De Lecture**.

Sarah The Caterpillar Reading Book 1-10
ISBN - 13: 978-0993902215   (MVM)
ISBN - 10: 0993902219   (MVM)

Contact:
+ MacAdam Visual Media +
macadamvisualmedia.com
macadamvisualmedia@gmail.com
902-961-2348

Louise Pierlot MacAdam
8837 West St. Peters
Morell PEI Canada
C0A 1S0

Sarah The Caterpillar
Integrated Reading Program

Sarah The Caterpillar Reading Book
Sarah The Caterpillar Workbook
Sarah The Caterpillar Key Words Book
My Pictures and Stories Workbook

Sarah The Caterpillar is an integrated learn to read program. It is useful for all children learning to read at approximately the grade one level. The program is particularly directed to children having issues in learning to read due to difficulties focusing, remembering letters, letter groups, words, and differentiating phonemes. It is a simple, straightforward program easily used by parent, teacher and child.

The program has approximately 230 words and derived words vocabulary. The **Reading Book** is made up of 40 short stories, following the story of Sarah the caterpillar, Sam the spider and Theodora the bee as they go through a season and their various changes of life and has a happy ending. The **Workbook** follows the **Reading Book** with 40 lessons corresponding to the 40 stories in the **Reading Book**. The **Key Words Book** is an essential aid to both the **Reading Book** and the **Workbook**. The **My Pictures and Stories Workbook** is a valuable supplement to the program.

Integrated Reading Program Outline

The program is integrated in that the vocabulary that appears in the stories of the **Reading Book** is the basis for the exercises in the **Workbook**. A principle feature of the program is that the vocabulary is limited to only those words that appear in a particular story and any stories that precede that story. This is essential in particular for children who have difficulties to focus, to remember letters, sounds and words, and to differentiate phonemes visually, as single letters or letter groups.

The stories and lessons are designed to be short and simple, to promote success and keeping in mind a child's possible struggles. Progress is built on an incremental building of vocabulary, repetition in using the same words in different sentences patterns in the **Reading Book**, and short repetitive exercises in the **Workbook** that present with as much variation as possible, within the limits imposed by the restricted vocabulary.

The Reading Book

Each story is four pages long. The vocabulary is limited to the words of the story and the preceding stories. The sentences are structured using only the words that have been introduced in the same or preceding stories. The words are used frequently and repeated often in sentences of different lengths and variations.

Story 1 introduces these five words: **Sarah there the is caterpillar**.
Story 2 adds two more words: **Sam spider**.
Story 3 adds no new words, rather focusing on keeping the child engaged and reinforcing the words she has already learned.
Example: **Story 3** - page 4 (last page):   **There is Sarah.**
    There is Sarah the caterpillar.
    There is Sam.
    There is Sam the spider.

The book continues on in this manner, in that 1-5 words are added in each story up to story 26. In later stories larger numbers of words or derived words are added in each successive story. At the beginning of the program the child learns the words by sight and repetition, relying on the parent's or teacher's assistance to sound out the words. As the child makes progress by rereading the stories and completing the exercises in the **Workbook**, she becomes able to successfully sound out letters, and recognize phonemic groups and words on her own.

The Workbook

Each story in the **Reading Book** has an accompanying lesson in the **Workbook**, using only the vocabulary of the story and the preceding stories. The first three exercises are based on reading, speaking and writing the phonetic sounds in a variey of ways. The fourth is a reading for meaning exercise based on the story and its vocabulary.

Further material is provided in each lesson including script and cursive writing, drawing, tracing and colouring. The purpose of the writing exercises is for practice; in the case of the cursive writing exercises, if it is decided that the child will not do them, she may be encouraged to read the cursive writing for awareness and knowledge. In some schools of thought, the child is introduced to cursive writing at the grade one level without having been first taught script writing. The drawing, tracing and colouring exercises are intended as a pleasant finale to the lesson to promote fine hand movement and control for handwriting, and to encourage creativity. The parent or teacher may use all or part of these extra exercises, according to the needs and capacities of the child.

The Key Word Book

The **Key Word Book** is an integral part of the program. The **Key Words** are particularly chosen words used to assist the child to recall the sounds of vowels and of phoneme groups composed of several letters. Each phoneme has its own framed accompanying image, named with the phoneme underlined. The phoneme also appears underlined in large print in the upper right hand corner of each box.

The **Key Word** images are printed in two sizes on light weight card stock. The small images are intended to be removed from the book one full page at a time (without cutting) to use as reference in front of the child while she is reading the **Sarah The Caterpillar Reading Book** and working in the **Workbook**. The phonemes are presented more or less in order of their appearance in the **Reading Book** and **Workbook**.

The large images are intended to be mounted on the wall, one compete page at a time (without cutting) as the child is introduced to the phonemes in the program. As the child makes progress through the program, another page of the large images is to be added to the wall next to the previous page. In this way the child will have a gentle reminder throughout the day outside of lesson time, of the phonemes she is learning.

How To Use The Key Words

The **Key Words** are used as an aid while the child is reading in the **Reading Book** or doing exercises in the **Workbook.**
A child may have difficulty in two ways to recognize a phoneme:
1. She does not recall the sound of the phoneme
2. She does not see the letter group as forming a single sound ie: as **ing** in the **Key Word king**
The child needs practice and help to recall that the letters **ing** together make a particular sound which is not the same as seeing the letters seperately each with their own individual sound - i, n, and g

In the case where the child is having difficulty to recall the sound of a vowel or a phoneme, the parent or teacher directs the child to look at the **Key Word** image for the particular phoneme in question, without saying the phoneme. The image accompanied by the underlined phoneme assists the child to remember the phoneme by herself and to see the letters of the phoneme as a group making its own sound. This process should be repeated each time the child has difficulty recognizing and recalling the phoneme.

As well as appearing in the **Key Word Book,**
the **Key Words** are provided in the small format in the **Workbook** for convenience.

Suggested Use of the Program:

Day One:
1. Have the child read the first story in the **Reading Book**, assisting her as needed, taking enough time to help her sound out the words, or to guide her in following the words. If helpful, use a pointer (pencil) to indicate each word as she reads or to point to letters and phoneme groups as she sounds them out. The child is encouraged to recognize the words by sight, and to sound out the words, with help if required when she doesn't recognize the words.

2. In the **Workbook**, have the child do Exercise A and B in Lesson One. Have her read, speak and write as indicated in each exercise.

3. Have the child go over the phoneme practice page. This is the illustrated page with letters and phonemes written into the artwork. Use a pointer/pencil as needed to keep her on track. Encourage her to use the pointer herself when she is ready.

4. Have the child go to the last page in the lesson and do the drawing.

   Note: Each learning session including the **Reading Book** and **Workbook** has the aim to be finished in about 20 minutes. This does not include the time spent for the drawing work at the end.

Day Two:
1. Have the child reread the first story in the **Reading Book**, helping as needed in the same manner as above.

2. In the **Workbook**, have the child do exercises C and D in Lesson One, encouraging her to read, speak and write as indicated in the exercise.

3. Have the child go over the phoneme practice page again, using the pointer as needed, or have her use the pointer while you watch.

4. Have the child do one of the writing exercises, either script or cursive - or both if the child is interested. She can begin by tracing the letters, using pencil, pen or marker - using whichever she finds comfortable. The cursive writing is included so the child begins to recognize it and occasionally practice it as she wishes. She might begin by tracing the letters, and then move on to forming her own letters in the following lessons.

   Note: Again, the learning session is intended to be finished in about 20 minutes. This does not include the time spent for the writing exercise.

Day Three
Move on to the second story in the **Reading Book** and Lesson Two in the **Workbook**, proceeding as outlined in **Day One** above.

Day Four
Proceed as for **Day Two** to complete Lesson Two: reread the second story in the **Reading Book**, do Exercises C and D, the phoneme practice page and the writing practice in Lesson Two of the **Workbook.**

Note: Some of the lessons in the **Workbook** have a page with a drawing for tracing. These are provided as supplementary work if the child is interested, or could be done in place of the drawing.

My Pictures and Stories

My Pictures and Stories is a valuable supplement to the program. It fosters interest in reading, writing, handwriting, drawing and creativity. This practice can be continued as the child progresses into the next grades. Over time the child often develops her own serialized stories.

Using My Pictures and Stories

The parent or teacher can use the **My Picures and Stories Workbook** or use a large scribbler in which the left hand pages are blank and the right hand pages are lined. On the first day the child draws anything she would like, using pencil, pen, marker or whatever she wishes. On the second day the child is asked to talk about her drawing and then to form a correct sentence about her drawing. This is written on the right hand page, using double spacing. If the child cannot do this, the parent or teacher should write it out for her, leaving a double space below each line for the child to then copy the sentence. As the child progresses in reading and writing, she should use two or more sentences to describe the drawing. As the stories become longer, the child can write them out on a separate piece of paper, ask for it to be checked over for errors, and then copy the corrected story into her scribbler.

Comments and Tips:

The parent or teacher should feel free to use as much or as little of the program as they find useful in the case of each child. Some children may learn quickly and the parent or teacher will find the program too repetitive for the child's capacity. Other children may need to proceed more slowly (sometimes much more slowly) with lessons kept short, according to the capacity of the child.

It is important to end each lesson on a note of success, before the point of frustration. In some cases this may necessitate that the lesson be very short. The parent or teacher will judge the ability of each child, and where lies her point of frustration. In such cases, one can try to do two or three short sessions in the day, if this works. Even five to ten minutes a day, carried out consistently every day will result in progress. If the child is doing what you ask even for a short lesson, count this as success.

The age of the child has a lot of bearing on brain readiness to read, the ability to focus and to use a pen, pencil or marker. This may mean that lessons need to be kept short, but should not necessarily be given up. It is in regular repetition that the neural pathways in the brain are strengthened, even and especially where the child is having difficulties. The child herself learns through short consistant appropriate lessons, how to succeed and how to deal with any difficulties and frustrations in learning. Half the battle is won if the child knows that she **is expected to** and and **is able to** complete the work each day, or on a regular basis, and that **she knows that she can succeed** in the daily lesson.

Thoughts To Keep In Mind:

"You cannot ask a child to do what she **is not** able, but you **must** ask the child to do what she **is** able to do."

"End as much as possible on a note of success, even if the lesson is short...or very short!"

"Stop before the point of frustration."

These are guidelines for the parent or teacher working with a child who is having difficulties. It may not seem that these guidelines even get a chance to be followed, especially when beginning lessons, trying to get started, or when the whole procedure is a battle zone, but if these guidelines are kept in mind, they can be key to success. Sometimes as adults we tend to push forward when there is a success - when we should instead possibly pull back and end the lesson on that **note of success**!

Sarah

one

1

one

Sarah.

Sarah the caterpillar.

There is Sarah.

There is Sarah the caterpillar.

There is Sarah.

There is the caterpillar.

There is Sarah the caterpillar.

Sam

two

2

two

Sam.

Sam the spider.

There is Sam the spider.

There is Sam

There is the spider.

There is Sam the spider.

Sarah and Sam

three

3

three

New Words

There aren't any!

Sarah.
Sarah the caterpillar.

Sam.

Sam the spider.

There is Sarah.

There is Sam.

There is the caterpillar.

There is the spider.

There is Sarah.

There is Sarah the caterpillar.

There is Sam.

There is Sam the spider.

The Caterpillar
and
The Spider

four

4

four

New Words	
and	a

There is Sarah.

Sarah is a caterpillar.

There is Sarah the caterpillar.

There is Sam.

Sam is a spider.

There is Sam the spider.

There is Sarah.   There is Sam.
Sarah and Sam.   Sam and Sarah.

Sam is a spider.

Sarah is a caterpillar.

Sam the spider.

Sarah the caterpillar.

Sarah is Drinking

five

5

five

There is Sarah the caterpillar.

Sarah is a caterpillar.

There is the water.
Sarah is drinking.
The caterpillar is drinking.

The caterpillar is drinking.
The caterpillar is drinking water.

There is the water.
There is the caterpillar.
There is Sarah the caterpillar.

Sarah is Shedding

six

6

six

<u>New Words</u>

climbing   shedding

new   shiny

There is Sarah.

There is the caterpillar.

There is Sarah the caterpillar.

Sarah is climbing.

The caterpillar is climbing.

Sarah the caterpillar is climbing.

Sarah is climbing.
The caterpillar is climbing.

There, the caterpillar is shedding.
There, Sarah the caterpillar is shedding.

There, Sarah is new.
The caterpillar is new.
Sarah the caterpillar is shiny new!

Sarah's Skin

seven

7

seven

New Words

skin   her

in   's

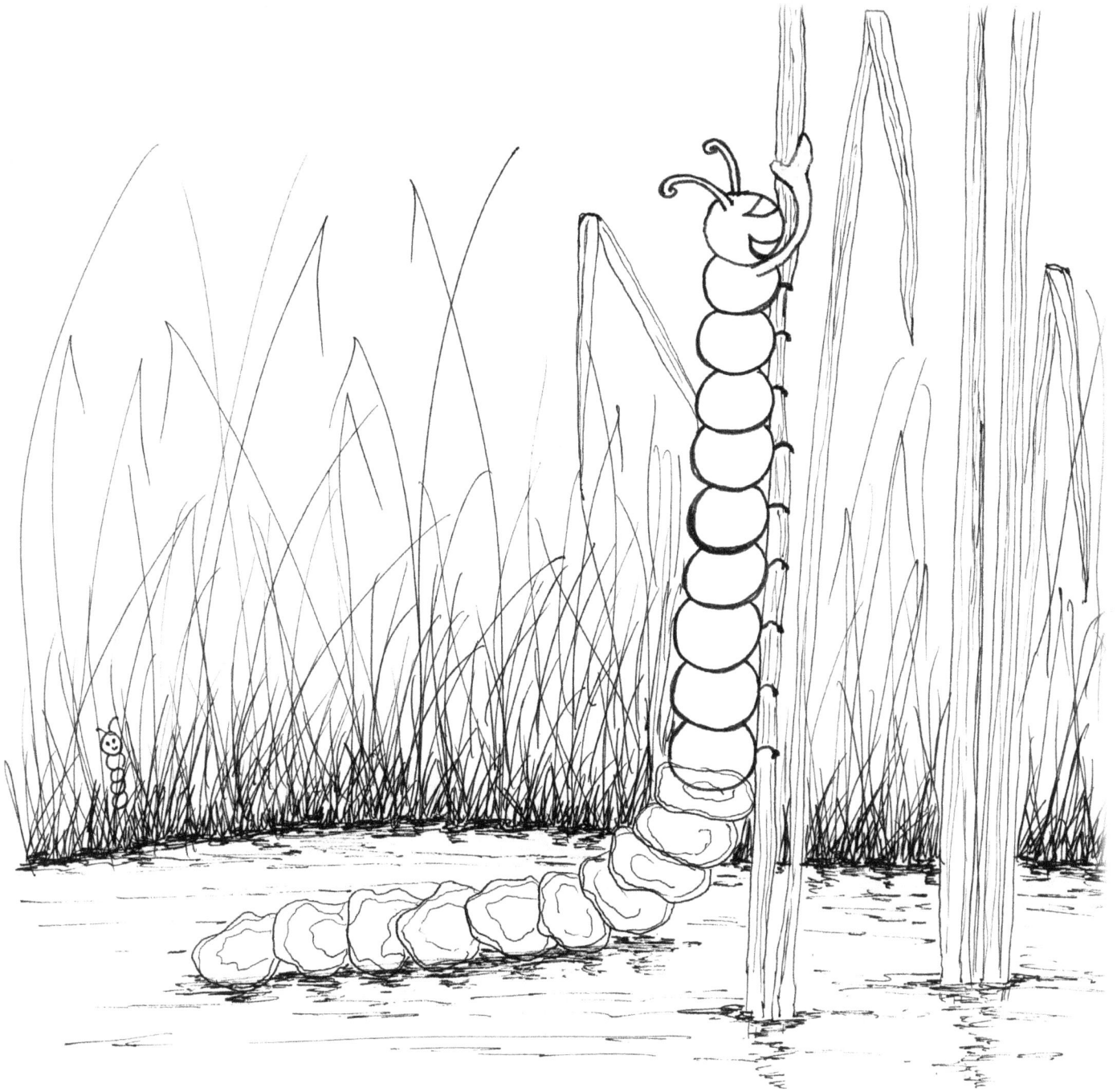

There is Sarah climbing.
There is Sarah shedding.

Sarah the caterpillar is climbing.
Sarah the caterpillar is shedding.

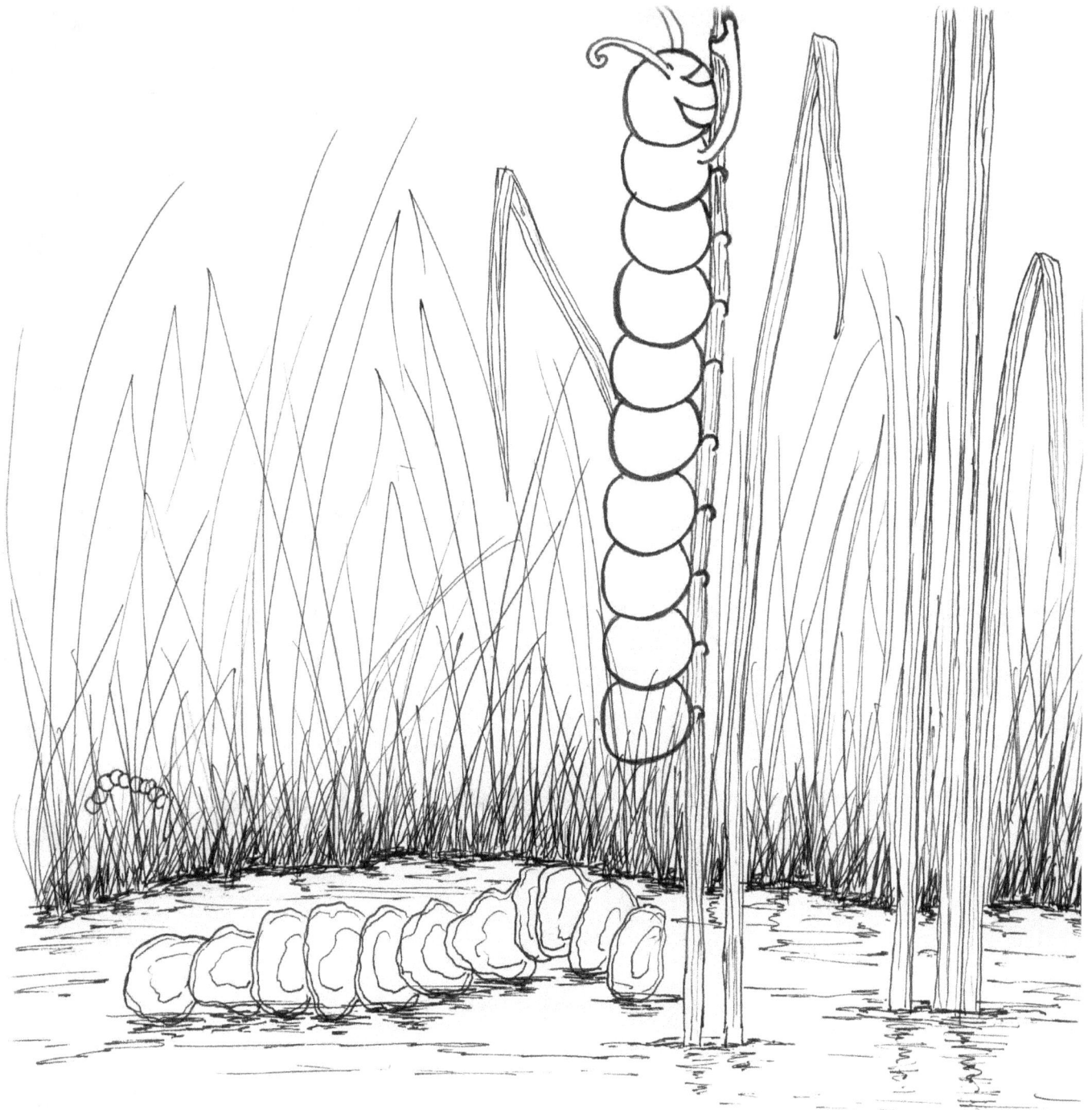

Sarah is shedding.

Sarah is shedding her skin.

There is the water.

There is the skin.

The skin is in the water.

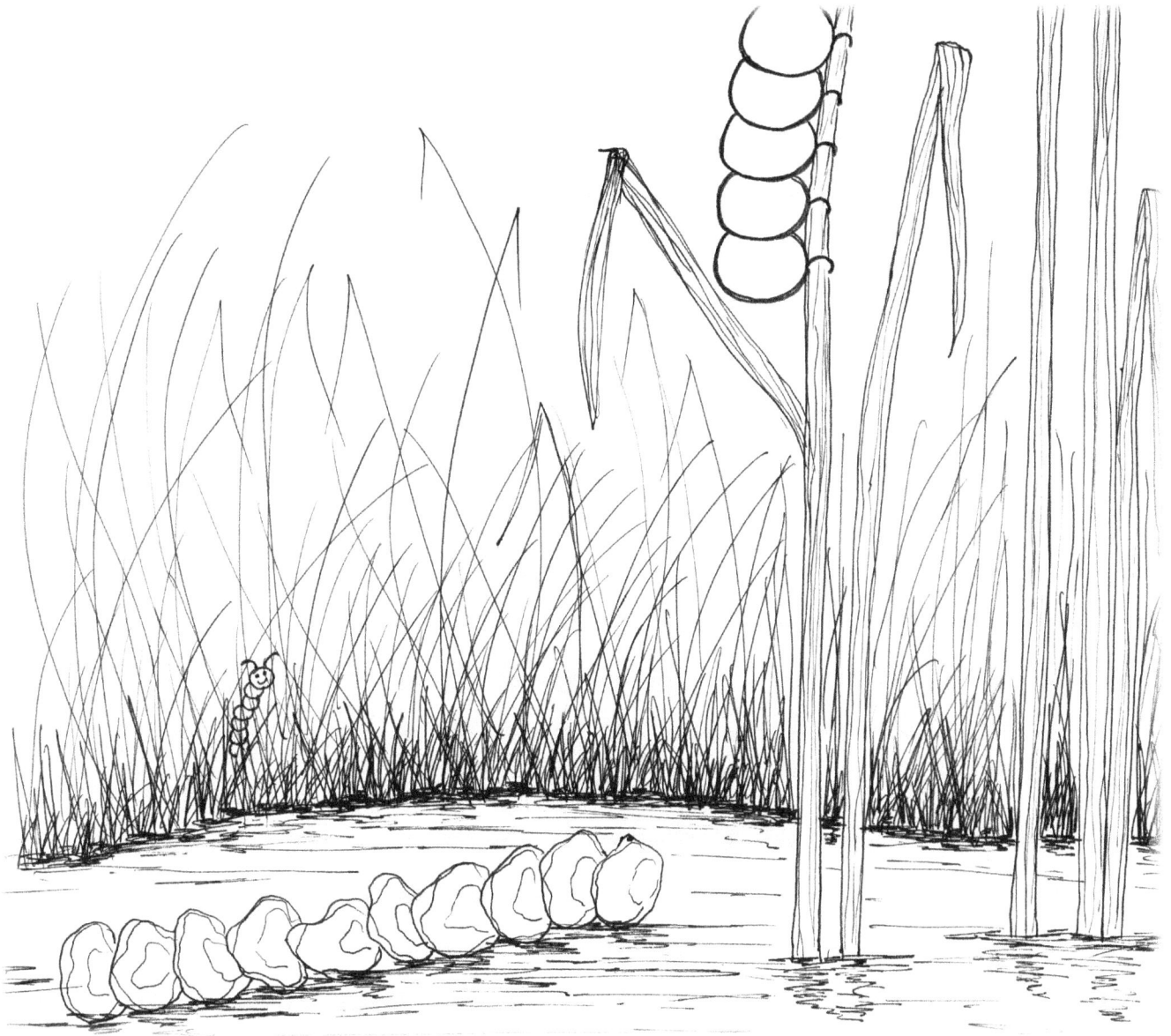

There is Sarah's skin.
The skin is in the water.
Sarah's skin is in the water.

Sarah is climbing.
Sarah the caterpillar is climbing.
Sarah the caterpillar is shiny new.

Sarah is shedding.

The caterpillar is shedding.

Sarah is new.

The caterpillar is shiny new!

There is the skin.

There is Sarah's skin.

The skin is in the water.

Sarah's skin is in the water.

7-4

Shiny New In The Road

eight

8

eight

New Words

all   road

There is Sarah.
There is the road.
There is Sarah in the road.

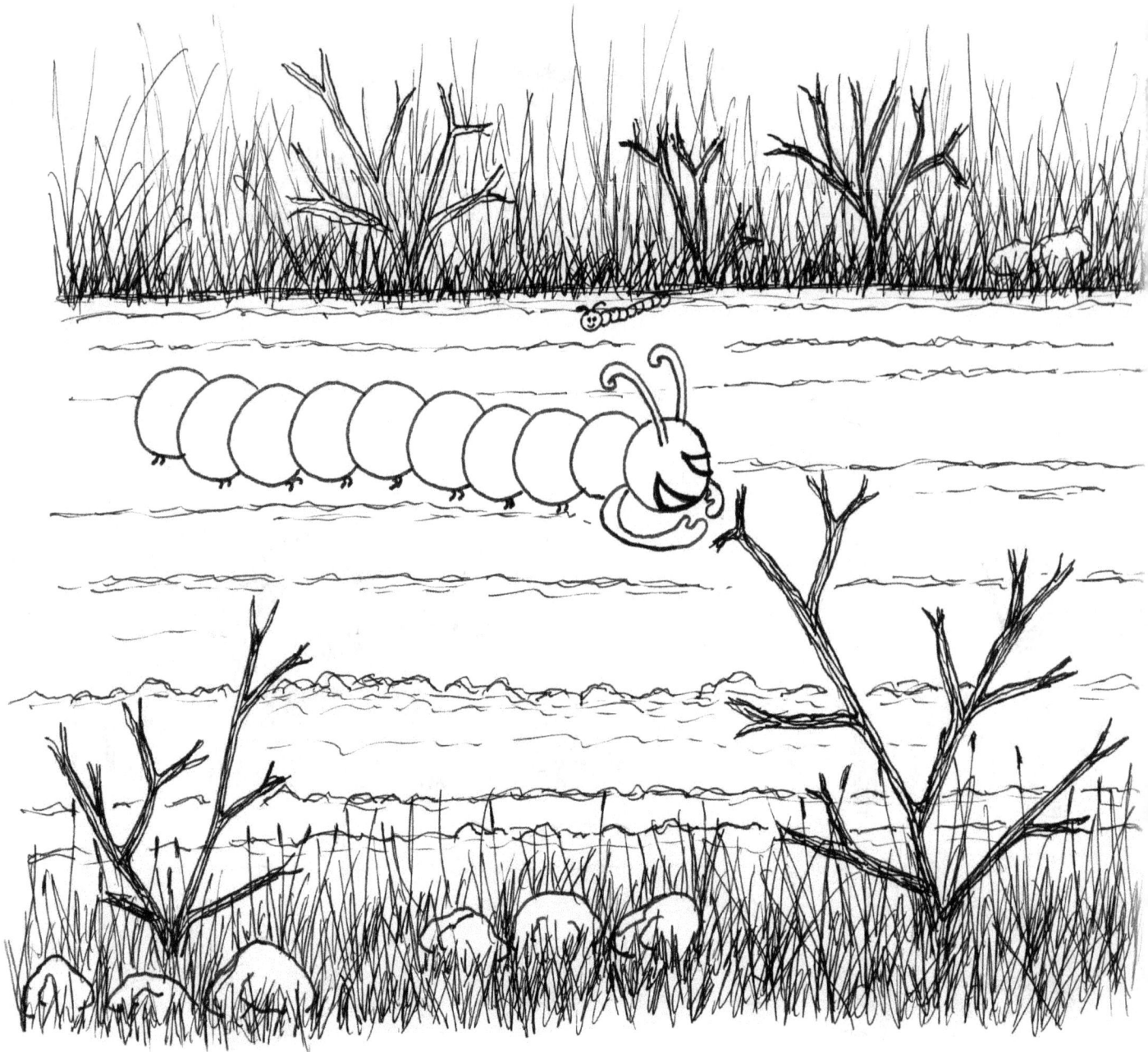

There is Sarah.
There is Sarah in the road.

Sarah is new.
Sarah is all shiny new.

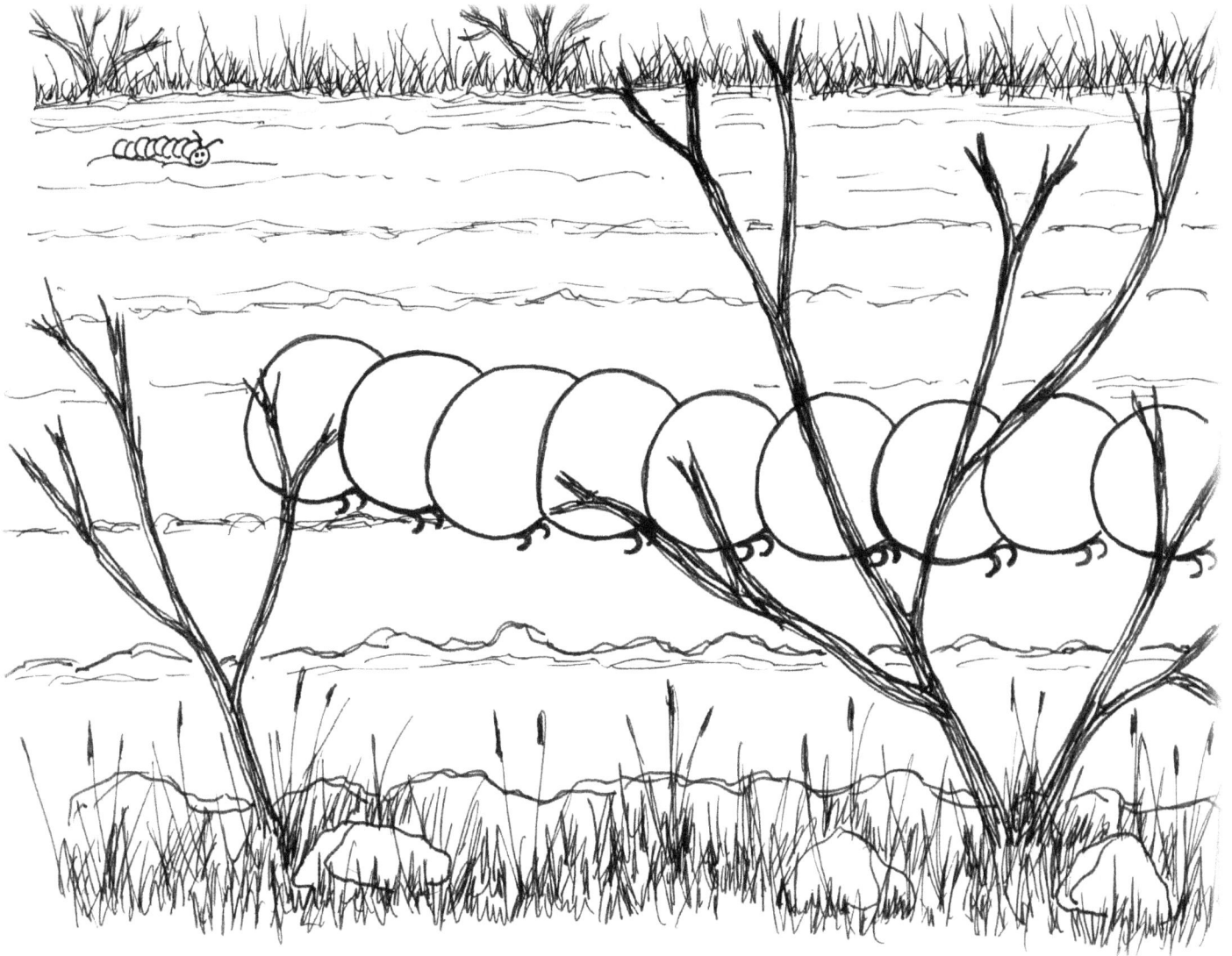

There is the road.
Sarah is in the road.

Sarah is all new.
Sarah is all shiny new in the road.
Hah! Hah! Hah!

There is Sarah.

There is the caterpillar.

Sarah the caterpillar is
all shiny new in the road.
Hah!   Hah!   Hah!

In The Road

nine

9

nine

New Words	
sees	drinks

There is Sam.
There is Sam the spider.

Sam sees Sarah.
Sarah sees Sam.

Sarah sees Sam.
Sam sees Sarah.

Sarah sees the water.
Sam sees the water.

Sarah drinks the water.
Sam drinks the water.

Sarah drinks the water in the road.
Sam drinks the water in the road.

Sam is drinking water.
Sam drinks the water in the road.

Sarah is drinking water.
Sarah drinks the water in the road.

Mud

ten

10

ten

New Words

mud   are

Sarah the caterpillar is in the road.
Sam the spider is in the road.
The water is in the road.

Sarah sees the water.
Sarah sees the mud.

Sam sees the water.
Sam sees the mud.

Sarah sees the water in the road.
Sarah sees the mud in the road.

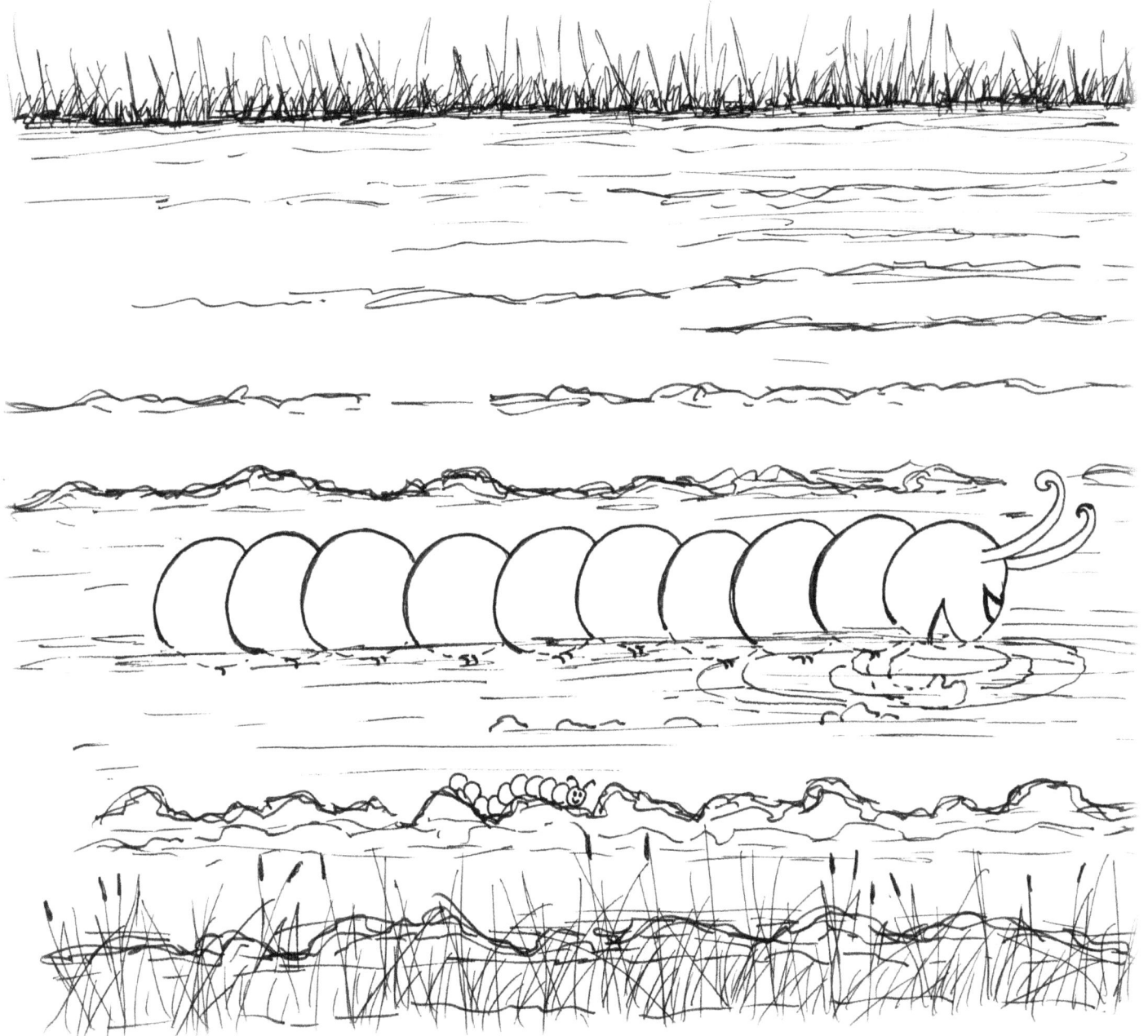

The water and the mud are in the road.
Sarah and Sam are in the road.

Sarah drinks the water in the road.
Sam drinks the water in the road.

There, the caterpillar is drinking.
There, the spider is drinking.

Sarah the caterpillar is drinking water.
Sam the spider is drinking water.

Word List
As they appear in the story.

1 there
is
Sarah
the
caterpillar

2 Sam
spider

3 No words

4 and
a

5 drinking
water

6 climbing
shedding
new
shiny

7 skin
her
in
's

8 all
road

9 sees
drinks

10 mud
are

11 playing
rolling

12 laughing

13 nose
everywhere
on
laughs
rolls

14 bee
Theodora
Bzzz

15 eating
not
because

16 rolled
leaves
eaten
enough
has

17 goes
flower
web
grass

18 sun
shining
drying

19 going
night
down
stars
dark

20 sleepy
sleeping

21 coming
morning
up
look

22 dew
everything
waking

23 he
she
it
they

24 dried
drunk
fly

25 tree
Bzzz'
bees
out
hive
of
flowers

26 hot
nectar
honey
cool
beats
beating
their
wings
making

27 working
looking
still
pollen
hard
for

28 putting
walking
wax
abdomen
abdomens
bees'
honeycomb
very

29 hungry
leaves
outside
insects
waiting
growing
under
mushroom
thread
lot
his
an
eats

30 eggs
   queen
   many
   larvae
   young
   small
   bigger
   biggest
   laying
   becoming
   feeding
   from

31 again
   plucks
   swinging
   gives
   listens
   Matilda
   wind
   another
   threads
   happy
   friend

32 hatch
   hatching
   big
   soon
   come
   now
   closing
   with
   cells
   will

33 stem
   friends
   mushrooms
   blowing
   field
   beautiful
   food
   stag beetle
   grasshopper
   firefly
   ant
   anthill
   day

34 slept
   now
   silk
   sac
   winding
   drop
   to
   cocoon
   around
   ball
   herself
   tired
   like

35 work
   when
   feed
   do
   more
   getting
   winter
   summer
   lay
   put

36 pass
   passes
   passing
   other
   time
   sleeps
   thunder
   storm
   thunderstorm
   after
   rain
   rains
   rainbow
   always
   lightening
   sometimes
   days
   nights

37 ready
   tiny
   listen
   pluck
   plucking
   find
   flies
   hear
   one
   spiderlings
   stems
   so

38 fast
   fall
   leave
   float
   floating
   away
   long
   longer
   ballooning

39 far
   carrying
   air
   watching
   fields
   webs
   wait

40 hole
   bit
   hatched
   butterfly
   any
   larve
   that
   glad
   be
   how
   by

www.ingramcontent.com/pod-product-compliance
Lightning Source LLC
Chambersburg PA
CBHW081523040426
42447CB00013B/3315